FLORIDA
The Sunshine State

Derek Miller, Debra Hess,
and Lori Wisenfeld

Cavendish
Square
New York

Published in 2019 by Cavendish Square Publishing, LLC
243 5th Avenue, Suite 136, New York, NY 10016
Copyright © 2019 by Cavendish Square Publishing, LLC

Website: cavendishsq.com

This publication represents the opinions and views of the author based on his or her personal experience, knowledge, and research. The information in this book serves as a general guide only. The author and publisher have used their best efforts in preparing this book and disclaim liability rising directly or indirectly from the use and application of this book. All websites were available and accurate when this book was sent to press.

Library of Congress Cataloging-in-Publication Data

Names: Miller, Derek, author. | Hess, Debra, author. | Wiesenfeld, Lori P., author.
Title: Florida / Derek Miller, Debra Hess, and Lori P. Wiesenfeld.
Description: New York : Cavendish Square, 2019 | Series: It's my state! (Fourth edition) |
Includes bibliographical references and index. | Audience: Grades 3-5.
Identifiers: LCCN 2017048031 (print) | LCCN 2017048905 (ebook) | ISBN 9781502626264
(library bound) | ISBN 9781502626202 (ebook) | ISBN 9781502644374 (pbk.)
Subjects: LCSH: Florida--Juvenile literature.
Classification: LCC F311.3 (ebook) | LCC F311.3 .H47 2019 (print) | DDC 975.9--dc23
LC record available at https://lccn.loc.gov/2017048031

Editorial Director: David McNamara
Editor: Caitlyn Miller
Copy Editor: Nathan Heidelberger
Associate Art Director: Alan Sliwinski
Designer: Jessica Nevins
Production Coordinator: Karol Szymczuk
Photo Research: J8 Media

Printed in the United States of America

It's My STATE!

Table of Contents

SNAPSHOT
FLORIDA

The Sunshine State

State Seal

The state seal is the size of a silver dollar. In the foreground, there is a Native American woman scattering flowers. There is also a sabal palmetto, the state tree. In the background, the sun's rays break over the horizon and a steamboat floats on the water.

State Flag

Florida's flag features the state seal in the middle on a white background. The red X behind the seal was added in 1900. It was feared the flag looked like a plain white flag of surrender hanging on a flagpole without it. Historians debate whether the red X was also meant to call to mind a similar design on either the Confederate flag or the flag of the Spanish Empire that used to rule Florida.

Statehood

March 3, 1845

Population

20,984,400
(2017 census estimate)

Capital

Tallahassee

HISTORICAL EVENTS TIMELINE

1513

Spanish explorer Juan Ponce de León is the first European to set foot in present-day Florida.

1539

Spanish **conquistador** Hernando de Soto launches an armed invasion of Florida.

1565

The Spanish found Saint Augustine (or, as it was known then, San Augustín). It is the first successful European settlement in Florida.

State Flower

Orange Blossom

Florida's state flower is the orange blossom. This white flower appears on orange trees, which are grown across the state for their fruit. Orange blossoms are treasured for their fragrant, appealing smell. They are even used to make perfumes.

State Tree

Sabal Palmetto

The sabal palmetto is a soaring palm tree that can grow to heights of 83 feet (25 meters). It is the state tree. The sabal palmetto is found across most of Florida because it is quite hardy. The sabal palmetto is also known as the cabbage palmetto or cabbage palm because its buds are edible. However, it is most frequently used by humans as an ornamental tree for landscaping.

1819

Spain agrees to sell Florida to the United States.

1845

Florida becomes the twenty-seventh state.

1861

Florida leaves the Union and joins the Confederacy.

State Bird
Mockingbird

State Reptile
American Alligator

Many states have an official state reptile, but perhaps no state is as closely associated with its reptile as Florida is. The American alligator (*Alligator mississippiensis*) serves as a recognizable symbol for the Sunshine State. This is in part because alligators are the University of Florida's official mascot. Alligators can be found in every county in the state.

1969

The first two humans to set foot on the moon are transported there from Florida by *Apollo 11*.

1971

Walt Disney World opens to the public.

1992

Hurricane Andrew sweeps through Florida. The storm results in sixty-five deaths nationwide and more than $25 billion in damages.

State Song

"Swanee River"

The state song of Florida is "Old Folks at Home." The song is also known as "Swanee River." Written in 1851, the song tells the story of a person born near the Suwannee River in northern Florida who longs to go home. In 2008, a newly composed song called "Florida, Where the Sawgrass Meets the Sky" was adopted as the state anthem. As a result, Florida has a state song and a state anthem.

State Animal

Florida Panther

State Beverage

Orange Juice

CURRENT EVENTS TIMELINE

2011

The Space Shuttle program comes to an end at the Kennedy Space Center.

2013

Florida marks the five-hundredth anniversary of the landing of Juan Ponce de León with celebrations called Viva Florida 500.

2018

Many Florida students come together to protest gun violence after a mass shooting at Stoneman Douglas High School.

Panama City Beach boasts more than three
hundred sunny days a year.

1 Geography

Florida is famous for its white beaches and sparkling blue water. Its natural beauty has driven many people to move to the state and make their new home there. But there's more to Florida than its coasts. The state is also home to the Everglades—a tropical wetland filled with diverse plants and animals. And in the north of the state, beaches and swamps give way to scenic rolling hills and pine forests.

The Geological Regions of Florida

Florida is the southernmost state in the **continental United States** (Hawaii is farther south). A large part of Florida is a **peninsula** that projects about 400 miles (640 kilometers) into the sea. A peninsula is land that is surrounded by water on three sides. The northern part of Florida runs along the shore of the Gulf of Mexico. It is called the Panhandle because it is shaped like the handle of a frying pan. The southern tip of the state is less than 100 miles (160 km) from Cuba.

FAST FACT

As the United States tried to land a man on the moon for the first time, NASA's work was centered in Florida. The state's geography and climate made it well-suited to the mission. Rockets could be launched over the Atlantic Ocean in an area with few people. This made it less likely debris would injure people on the ground. Also, the state's year-round warm weather made it possible for work to take place in all four seasons.

Florida, detailed below and shaded above, borders Alabama and Georgia.

Florida's current size and shape are a result of millions of years of **geological** change. Large pieces of rock, called plates, lie beneath Earth's surface. Over time, these plates move around, combining and breaking landmasses, and shaping the features of Earth's surface. Erosion changed Florida's shape and landscape. (Erosion is the process of being worn away by wind, rain, and water current.) Dirt, sand, shells, and rocks brought by the wind and ocean currents also shaped parts of Florida. Over time, sea creatures such as coral and mollusks lived and died on the coasts of Florida. Their remains hardened into rocks and minerals and added mass to Florida's coasts.

One million years ago, Earth's climate turned much colder. Large amounts of ocean water turned into ice. Large masses of ice called glaciers covered much of the planet. As a result, the water level in the oceans sank. At that time, the land that is now Florida was twice its current size. When this ice age ended, water levels rose. Much of Florida's land was covered by water. The rise in water levels also formed swamps.

The Florida peninsula lies on the relatively flat land formation called the Florida Platform. The highest point in the entire state is Britton Hill in the north. It is only 345 feet (105 meters) high. It is the lowest high point of all fifty states. Florida has 53,625 square miles

(138,888 square kilometers) of land, making it the twenty-sixth-largest state in the country.

The area of Florida known as the Coastal Lowlands stretches around the coastal borders of the state. The lowlands are covered with forests of sabal palmetto and cypress. The best-known area of the Coastal Lowlands is the Everglades. The Everglades cover a large portion of the state, stretching from Lake Okeechobee, the state's largest lake, to the Gulf of Mexico. Mangrove trees, ferns, and a razor-sharp plant called saw grass cover much of this marshy wetland. The wildlife in the park includes alligators, waterfowl, and hundreds of kinds of frogs, turtles, and snakes.

Mangrove trees are a defining feature of the Everglades.

For many years, people considered the Everglades a worthless swamp. Developers began to drain the Everglades in order to use the land. They had dreams of building hotels and tourist resorts in this region. Wildlife was killed. Habitats were destroyed.

Starting in the 1930s, many nature enthusiasts, such as Ernest F. Coe, worked toward passing laws to protect the Everglades. In 1947, Marjory Stoneman Douglas wrote *The Everglades: River of Grass*. The book called attention to the wonders of the Everglades, begging the world to preserve

The Everglades are federally protected land.

its sensitive ecosystem. Many plants and animals living there were endangered. Destroying their habitat would make them disappear forever. The efforts of the Everglades' supporters paid off in 1947. That year, President Harry Truman dedicated Everglades National Park,

Walt Disney World and Other Top Attractions

When Walt Disney World first opened, it consisted of Magic Kingdom and three resorts. However, it was never a given that Walt Disney would select Orlando, Florida, as the site of his theme park. Disney looked at many places before deciding that Florida would be the home of Mickey, Minnie, and Cinderella's Castle. He selected Orlando because there was a lot of land available for purchase—and because he knew that between Florida's airports and highways, visitors from all over would be able to get to his park easily. Over the years, Disney World has grown, offering visitors exciting new parks like Disney's Animal Kingdom and Epcot (a name that stands for Experimental Prototype Community of Tomorrow).

Disney was right to think Florida would be a great location for his park. Of course, Florida has many tourist attractions beyond Walt Disney World that make use of the state's appealing features. Racing fans flock to Daytona International Speedway, a venue that can hold more than one hundred thousand people. Aside from Disney, other top theme parks in Florida include the Wizarding World of Harry Potter, Universal Studios Orlando, and SeaWorld Orlando. And when it comes to outdoor recreation, Florida's nearly 1,000 miles (1,609 km) of beaches are a major draw!

After the sun sets, fireworks shows draw crowds to Disney parks.

protecting a large portion of the region—and the wildlife within it—from development.

The southernmost parts of the state are called the Florida Keys. This chain of islands is 110 miles (177 km) long. It stretches from Biscayne Bay—located on the southeastern coast of Florida—southwest, toward the Gulf of Mexico. The only living coral reef in the continental United States is here. Some of the islands also have tropical forests. But many people live on the islands in close-knit communities. Bridges and the Overseas Highway connect most of the islands. However, some islands can be reached only by boat. Key West, on the western end of the islands, is the southernmost city in the continental United States.

The Gulf of Mexico and the Florida Keys

Florida's highest points rise from the sea with hilly pine forests in the northwestern corner of the state. The Western Highlands are low compared to many other parts of the United States. Rolling hills and small villages surround the highlands.

East of the Western Highlands and north of the Coastal Lowlands are the Marianna Lowlands. Hills and valleys make up this

Florida's Biggest Cities

(*Population numbers are from the US Census Bureau's 2017 projections for incorporated cities.*)

Jacksonville: population 892,062

At 840 square miles (2,176 sq km), Jacksonville is the largest city by landmass in the continental United States. It is nicknamed "The River City" because the Saint Johns River flows right through it. There are also many beaches, parks, and museums.

Miami: population 463,347

This vibrant city in southern Florida is known for its dynamic culture. Shopping, fishing, nightlife, art, and architecture are just some of the things residents and visitors enjoy. Miami is also one of the largest US cities with a Spanish-speaking majority.

Tampa: population 385,430

Located on the west coast of Florida near the Gulf of Mexico, Tampa is a city that is growing fast. Thanks to a strong economy, outdoor activities, and major sports teams, Tampa is one of the most popular places to live in the Southeast.

Orlando: population 280,257

Orlando is one of the most popular tourist destinations in the United States. It is home to many theme parks, including Walt Disney World, Universal Studios, and SeaWorld. The city is called "The Theme Park Capital of the World."

Saint Petersburg: population 263,255

Saint Petersburg sits on a peninsula between the Gulf of Mexico and Tampa Bay. It is nicknamed "The Sunshine City," as it averages around 360 sunny days a year. Saint Petersburg has also become a popular retirement city for senior citizens.

Jacksonville

Miami

Hialeah: population 239,673

Hialeah, located northwest of Miami, is known for its high percentage of Cuban and Cuban American residents. Around 90 percent of its residents speak Spanish fluently.

Tallahassee: population 191,049

Tallahassee, the capital of Florida and the largest city on the Florida Panhandle, is a center for trade and agriculture. Two popular colleges, Florida State University and Florida A&M, are located in Tallahassee as well.

Port Saint Lucie: population 189,344

Port Saint Lucie is a popular destination for golfers. The Professional Golfers' Association (PGA) Village includes fifty-four holes of golf, a golf museum, and a learning center. The city is also home to the New York Mets' spring training camp.

Tampa

Cape Coral: population 183,365

Located in southwestern Florida, Cape Coral's residents have a view of the Gulf of Mexico. Cape Coral attracts tourists with family-friendly attractions and their more than 400 miles (645 km) of canals.

Fort Lauderdale: population 180,072

Fort Lauderdale is named for several forts that the United States built during the Second Seminole War in 1838. They were named after Major William Lauderdale. Today, the city is known for its many waterways, and it is often called "The Venice of America."

Tallahassee

The Suwannee River lends its name to Florida's state song, "Swanee River."

section of Florida, where many people still farm. The Tallahassee Hills lie farther east. Oak and pine trees cover the hills, which slope toward the famous Suwannee River to the east. The Suwannee River flows south from the Okefenokee Swamp in Georgia, down through parts of Florida, and into the Gulf of Mexico. In the center of the Florida peninsula is a 250-mile (400 km) stretch of land known as the Central Highlands. Flat grassy plains, citrus groves, and lakeside communities make up this area.

Climate

Florida's climate is hot and humid. Heavy rains fall from April to November. As one native Floridian said of the rain and humidity, "We may not have to deal with cold and snow, but Florida is a bad hair state." Even though Florida is warm year-round, record highs are quite low. The hottest temperature recorded in Florida is just 109 degrees Fahrenheit (42.8 degrees Celsius). Compare that to the record high of 111°F (43.9°C) in the northern state of Pennsylvania.

The state has the longest coastline of any US state except Alaska. When temperatures soar, there are plenty of coastal places to swim and cool off.

This NASA image shows a hurricane headed toward Florida.

Floridians do not have to deal with freezing temperatures and snowstorms, but from the beginning of June to the end of November, they have to worry about hurricanes. A hurricane is a tropical storm with wind speeds of at least 74 miles per hour (119 kilometers per hour). A hurricane begins over an ocean, where the sun warms the surface of the water and causes the water to evaporate. The evaporated water floats into the air and forms thunderclouds. The rotation of Earth sends these storm clouds spinning toward land. When a hurricane hits a developed area, the flooding can destroy buildings and kill people.

More hurricanes strike Florida than any other state. The damage can be massive. In 1992, Hurricane Andrew caused sixty-five deaths nationwide and destruction that totaled $25 billion. Floridians worked together with people from other parts of the country to repair and rebuild their communities.

Wildlife

More than ninety species of mammals live in different parts of the state, including the black bear, panther, gray fox, and otter. Florida's waters are known for their abundant fish and shellfish. The coastal waters are filled with shrimp, oysters, crabs, scallops, clams, conchs, and crayfish. Bass and catfish swim in the freshwater lakes and rivers. The oceans are full of grouper, mackerel, marlin, and trout. More than one thousand species of fish have been identified in Florida's waters.

Fish are not the only animals you will find in the water. Bottlenose dolphins inhabit Florida's coastal waters. But swimming with or feeding dolphins can be dangerous for both humans and animals. When traveling through the swamp, animals—including humans—must look out for alligators lurking in the waters.

Five hundred species of wild birds soar over Florida's waters and land. These include

Hurricane Andrew caused devastating damage in 1992.

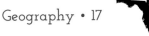

The Creation of Florida

Early explorers were impressed by Florida's **bounty**. One of the earliest written records describing Florida comes from Rodrigo Rangel. He was the secretary of the second Spanish conquistador to set foot on Florida: Hernando de Soto. No firsthand source of Juan Ponce de León's first doomed expedition exists. Rangel reports that the Spanish were quite pleased by the bounty that Florida had to offer:

> The province of Apalache is very fertile and very abundant in supplies, with much corn and beans and squash, and diverse fruits, and many deer and many varieties of birds, and near the sea there are many and good fish, and it is a pleasant land although there are swamps; but they are firm because they are over sand.

Nevertheless, the swamps presented a serious problem for de Soto's expedition. Historical records are full of difficulties they caused. Crossing the swamps was a slow process. Another record describes the relief of one group of men when they came upon a field of corn after having run out of supplies in a swamp:

> Having marched six leagues, they found [de Soto] encamped in some very beautiful valleys having large maize [corn] fields, so productive that each stalk had three or four ears, some of which they gathered while mounted on their horses, in order to appease their hunger. They ate them raw, giving thanks to God, our Lord, for having **succored** them with such abundance, for to the needy anything seems a great deal.

Hernando de Soto made a perilous but rewarding journey through Florida.

The shape of Florida changed permanently in 1822. This map shows what it looked like before that, with a longer panhandle.

Once the Spanish conquered the new land of Florida, its borders looked very different from its modern ones. The Panhandle was much larger. It stretched north through modern-day Georgia to the Savannah River, which forms the border of South Carolina. It also stretched west to the Mississippi River. It included the current coasts of Alabama, Mississippi, and parts of Louisiana.

Over time, the Spanish gave up control of parts of the Panhandle. Florida shrank to its current size. When Florida was organized as a territory of the United States in 1822, it had its current shape. In 1845, it was admitted as a state. Florida's borders have not changed since.

Bottlenose dolphins can live past the age of fifty!

quail, cuckoos, ospreys, pelicans, woodpeckers, robins, pigeons, storks, and bald eagles. On the water, you might see herons, ducks, ibis, egrets, or flamingos. Wild turkeys also roam across some of Florida's woodlands and open forests. Human activity and the resulting changes to the environment almost completely killed off some of these birds.

The bald eagle, a well-known symbol of the United States, thrives in the state, under a careful state management plan, after being removed from the federal threatened species list in 2007. (If an animal or plant is threatened, that means it is likely to become endangered.) The flamingo, heron, egret, and ibis almost became extinct in the 1800s after hunters killed them for their feathers. These feathers were then sold to hat makers. Today, places such as Everglades National Park protect these beautiful birds.

The wood stork and Florida manatee are examples of the state's endangered animals. Endangered animals once had large populations. Now only very few remain. Their numbers decreased when hunters killed them for skins, feathers, or food. Car accidents (or collisions with boats in the case of the manatee) and habitat destruction also reduced their populations. The federal government stepped in and listed these animals as endangered species.

Thousands of bald eagles make their homes in Florida.

Once an animal is listed as endangered, it is illegal to hunt that animal or harm it in any way. Some endangered animals are taken to protected places. Sometimes humans try to re-create the animals' natural habitat to help them live longer and breed. The Everglades is home to many endangered animals. Through the efforts of Floridians and nature lovers across the country, many endangered animals and plants have had a chance to increase their numbers and survive.

The Future of Florida

As Florida tries to save its many endangered plants and animals, there is another threat looming in the future. Climate change—the rise of temperatures around the globe—threatens to melt ice on Earth's poles. This will cause an increase in sea level. Since so much of the state is just above sea level, even a small rise in water level could result in a disaster. Many local communities around Florida are preparing by building larger sea walls and requiring new houses to be built on higher ground.

FAST FACT
Florida is not just home to animals from the United States. Due to its tropical climate, pet snakes sometimes escape and go on to lead long lives in the wild. So many Burmese pythons have escaped in Florida that they now number in the thousands. Growing up to 18 feet (5.5 m) long, they devastate the local wildlife. Florida is attempting to eliminate them.

What Lives in Florida?

Flora

Holywood *Guaiacum sanctum* is a short tree that grows quite slowly. Its wood is exceptionally strong and heavy. When it is placed in water, it sinks instead of floating. As a result, it was often used to make important parts of ships that needed to be sturdy. In the United States, it only grows in South Florida and is threatened by habitat loss.

Key tree cactus

Key Tree Cactus *Pilosocereus robinii* is a large cactus that looks somewhat like a tree. Its trunk-like stem can grow to heights of 33 feet (10 m)! The Key tree cactus is found nowhere in the world except for the Florida Keys, an island chain at the southern tip of Florida.

Manchineel Tree *Hippomane mancinella* is a tree with fruit that looks similar to apples. This fruit has a number of nicknames, including "beach apple." In Spanish, the fruit is called "manzanilla de la muerte." This means "little apple of death." Fruit from the tree is highly poisonous. In fact, even the sap of the tree is poisonous. Some people think that it may have been used to poison the arrow that killed conquistador Juan Ponce de León.

Mrs. Britton's Shadow Witch Orchid *Ponthieva brittoniae* is a plant with beautiful greenish-white flowers. It is one of the southernmost orchids found in the United States. Orchids are a family of plants that have distinctive flowers.

Manchineel tree

Sargent's Cherry Palm *Pseudophoenix sargentii* is a palm tree that grows in Florida and countries nearby. It used to grow throughout South Florida. In the 1990s, a scientist discovered that there were only fifty trees left in the wild (on Elliott Key). From 1991 to 1994, botanists planted more than two hundred Sargent's cherry palm trees on thirteen sites across the Florida Keys.

Fauna

Crocodile The American crocodile is only found in South Florida in the United States. It looks very similar to its much more common cousin, the alligator. However, it is possible to tell them apart. The snout of a crocodile is much more V-shaped than the alligator's U-shaped snout.

American crocodile

Florida Panther There are just 120 to 230 wild panthers in Florida. These big cats can weigh up to 160 pounds (72.5 kilograms). Panthers are also called mountain lions, pumas, or cougars. Despite their size and their meat-only diet, there has not been a verified attack on a human by a panther in more than a hundred years.

Green Sea Turtles Five different species of sea turtles live in South Florida. All five are threatened or endangered due to humans. Trash in the ocean is a constant threat for turtles that eat it or become entangled in it. Their nesting grounds—sand beaches—are also often overrun by humans.

Florida panther

Manatees Manatees, or sea cows, are large aquatic mammals. They graze on underwater plants and live in the rivers and surrounding sea of South Florida. Manatees can grow up to 1,800 pounds (816 kg) and live to the age of sixty. The largest threat to the species is humans, especially the propellers of boats, which can severely injure them.

Manatee

Wood Stork This large bird has long legs that let it wade through shallow water. It mostly eats fish that it catches, and it builds large nests high up in trees for its eggs. In the United States, the wood stork is a threatened species because of its low population. However, there are large populations in Central and South America, so it is not threatened around the world.

Wood stork

Castillo de San Marcos is a fort built by the Spanish in the seventeenth century. Today, the Saint Augustine site is a national monument.

2 The History of Florida

Like most of the United States, Florida was first settled by Native Americans before the arrival of Europeans. But unlike the rest of the East Coast, it was the Spanish that first colonized Florida—not the English or Dutch. As a result, Florida's history is very different from most of the other states. It was the scene of fierce fighting between colonial powers as well as Native Americans and former slaves. Today, its unique history can still be seen across the state in place names and historic buildings that reveal the state's Spanish roots.

The First Floridians

No one knows exactly when the first humans arrived in today's Florida. But many experts think that Native Americans first reached the peninsula about twelve thousand years ago. They believe that some of them might have come from present-day Central and South America, crossing the water into what is now the southern part of the state. Other Native Americans might have come from the northwestern part of today's United States. These people might have

FAST FACT
During the American Revolution, East and West Florida remained loyal to the British Empire. Loyalists who wished to remain in the British Empire fled from the thirteen colonies into Florida. British armies marched out of Florida to invade Georgia to the north. George Washington sent American armies south to attack Florida but was unable to seize it.

Experts believe the
Ormond Indian Mound
dates to around 800 CE.

walked across the icy land bridge that used to exist between Asia and North America. Today, Alaska and Russia are separated by 50 miles (80 km) of water. But at one point a land bridge existed when sea levels were lower. Many experts think that all Native Americans can trace their ancestors to people who crossed this bridge.

Some large, dirt-covered mounds built by early Native Americans exist in the state today. They are called burial mounds. In many cases, the mounds contain human remains, religious artifacts, pottery, and jewelry.

It is estimated that when Europeans first arrived in the early sixteenth century, more than one hundred thousand Native Americans lived in present-day Florida. The Calusa and Tequesta tribes lived in the south. These tribes were hunters and gatherers. They speared fish for food, and they hunted bears, deer, and alligators with bows and arrows and clubs. They killed these animals for food and for clothing. The Timucua people, who lived in today's central and northeastern parts of the state, hunted animals and maintained farms. The Apalachee people, who lived in the northwest, were also hunters and farmers. Both groups farmed corn, beans, squash, and pumpkins.

The Conquistadors

The history of Europeans in Florida likely begins in 1513. That is the year that the Spanish are known to have first set foot on Florida. However, it is possible that some Europeans may have arrived earlier. If they did, there is no record of it. On April 2, 1513, Juan Ponce de León arrived at the new land with a group of men. It was on the day of Pascua Florida (Feast of the Flowers), which is Spain's Eastertime celebration. The explorer named the land "La Florida" in honor of the feast.

Ponce de León explored Florida and its surroundings before sailing to Puerto Rico. In 1521, the explorer returned with two hundred people, fifty horses, and many supplies. His idea was to colonize the land for Spain. But battles with Native Americans made this too difficult. Ponce de León was wounded in one of these battles and sailed to Cuba. There he died from his wound.

Despite this setback, explorers continued to come to the region. In 1539, another Spanish conquistador, Hernando de Soto, arrived in the area in search of silver and gold. He landed along the shore of what is now called Tampa Bay. But no great treasure awaited Hernando de Soto and his men. After exploring the southeast for several years, de Soto died from a fever in 1542 in present-day Louisiana. The rest of his expedition went to Mexico. In 1559, Tristán de Luna y Arellano led another Spanish expedition to colonize Florida. He founded a settlement at Pensacola Bay. However, it was

Conquistadors hoped to find riches in North America.

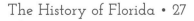

Native Americans in Florida

Florida was one of the first places discovered by the Europeans, but many people were living there long before the Spanish first landed. Native American tribes including the Creek, Choctaw, Calusa, and Timucua lived throughout the region. The Choctaw and the Creek lived in northwestern Florida, while the Timucua lived in northeastern and central Florida. There were several tribes in the south of the state, including the Calusa, Ais, Jeaga, and Tequesta. The variety of cultures from these different tribes is very important to the history of Florida.

The Native Americans of Florida lived off the land. Many tribes fished, hunted, and farmed. To fish, Native Americans made boats by hollowing out tree trunks. Some tribes were talented basket weavers, while others created **moccasins** and beaded dolls. A few tribes played a game called stickball, which was a lot like lacrosse. Many of the clothes across tribes were very similar—men wore breechcloths and women wore blouses and skirts.

When the Europeans came to Florida, the changes devastated the Native Americans who lived there. In the 1500s, there were between one hundred thousand and two hundred thousand Native Americans in the Florida area. But diseases and wars killed off many people, and by the 1700s, very few survived. The Timucua tribe actually went extinct, the last living tribe member dying in 1767. Another tribe, the Calusa, was very advanced. They beat the Spaniards in battle and created canals and man-made islands. Unfortunately, they nearly all died of disease. The few remaining tribe members disbanded.

This figure was made by a member of the Calusa tribe around 1000 CE.

The Seminole

The Seminole are descendants of the Creek tribe. A group of Creek people moved south from Alabama and Georgia to look for new land and to escape conflict between tribes. They called themselves "Seminole." It means "runaway" or "wild one."

After a series of three wars between the Seminole (joined by escaped African American slaves) and the United States government, the Seminole population decreased from around five thousand in the 1820s to less than three hundred in the 1850s. Today, several thousand Seminole people live in Florida.

Clans

Each Seminole born becomes a member of his or her mother's clan. Husbands then join their wives' clans. Each clan is named after an entity that shares the clan's traits. There are eight Seminole clans: Panther, Deer, Wind, Bear, Bigtown/Toad, Snake, Bird, and Otter.

Homes

The Seminole house was called a chickee. At first, the Seminole lived in log cabin–type homes. Because of conflict, though, it became necessary for them to have homes that were quick and easy to build, in case they needed to move. Chickees were made with wood frames and roofs made of palm leaves.

Clothing

Women generally wore long skirts and short blouses. Seminole women adorned themselves with jewelry made with glass beads. Young women wore as much jewelry as they could. Older women wore less. Seminole men wore long shirts, sometimes with leather belts, and wool turbans on their heads.

Transportation

The Seminole used canoes that were dug from cypress tree logs. They used these canoes to travel and to spear fish when hunting.

Fun Facts

Many cities in Florida get their names from Seminole words. "Hialeah" means "prairie," and "Ocala" means "spring."

The Seminole have long been known for their beautiful clothing.

A map from the sixteenth century shows the dwellings of Native Americans in Florida.

abandoned within two years after a series of misfortunes, including illness and lack of food.

Besides searching for treasure, new trade routes, and land to colonize, many Europeans came to the area to spread the Catholic religion. Priests came hoping to convert the Native Americans. The various tribes had their own religions, which were very different from Christianity. Many did not want to convert. They were often beaten or killed when they refused. Other Native Americans willingly converted. Still others, afraid and overpowered by the Europeans, practiced Christianity because they had no other choice.

During this time, many Spanish ships filled with treasures sailed the seas off the coast of present-day Florida. Most of them were headed back to Spain. The ships could carry a crew of about two hundred men. The chests of gold and silver were kept under guard in a room on the lower deck of the ship. But before they could reach Europe, many of these ships sank to the bottom of the ocean. Divers have found remains of some sunken treasure ships, while other vessels remain lost in the waters off Florida.

These treasure ships caused another problem: pirates. People sought their fortune by trying to capture ships laden with gold. In response, the Spanish built large, fortress-like ships called galleons. They also sent fleets of treasure ships rather than solitary ships. This also carried some risk, however. In 1715, a fleet of eleven Spanish ships sailed into a hurricane in the Caribbean. All of them sank, and more than a thousand people perished. In 2015, treasure hunters found just 350 coins from the disaster. They were valued at $4.5 million.

The Spanish were not the only Europeans interested in colonizing Florida. The French began exploring, trying to claim Florida

Juan Ponce de León was the first European known to have explored Florida. He and his men came ashore on April 2, 1513. This was during the Easter season—known as Pascua Florida in Spanish. In honor of the occasion, he named the land Florida. What he thought was an island turned out to be a vast new land.

In 1953, April 2 was declared Florida Day by the state to **commemorate** Ponce de León's discovery. Each year, the governor also has the power to declare the week leading up to April 2 as Pascua Florida Week.

Today, Ponce de León's legacy is bound up with the "Fountain of Youth." People around the world learn that the Spanish conquistador was looking for a legendary fountain that stopped people from aging. The story goes that on his search he stumbled upon Florida and claimed it for the Spanish.

In fact, this story is false. It was only years after Ponce de León's death that he was connected to the Fountain of Youth. This was done for political reasons, not because it was true. A Spanish chronicler wrote that Ponce de León heard about the fountain and went off looking for it. Even at the time, this was seen as a ridiculous idea. The chronicler was implying that Ponce de León was **gullible** and foolish.

It is much more likely that Ponce de León was simply searching for new lands and gold for the Spanish crown. In that case, his expedition was a success. And through Florida Day, it continues to be celebrated.

Ponce de León, Pascua Florida, and the Fountain of Youth

Florida Day celebrates the day that Juan Ponce de León landed in the state.

Sir Francis Drake
burned the city of
Saint Augustine in 1586.

for France. A French explorer named Jean Ribault traveled through the area in 1562. By 1564, the French had established Fort Caroline along the Saint Johns River, near present-day Jacksonville.

Spain did not want the French to gain control over Florida. Pedro Menéndez de Avilés was sent to Florida to remove the French and strengthen Spanish control over the land. In 1565, he established a settlement on the Atlantic coast called San Augustín (Saint Augustine). It was the first permanent European settlement in what would later become the United States. Menéndez de Avilés and his men killed most of the French settlers. They took Fort Caroline from the French and renamed it San Mateo.

The French fought back three years later, when Dominique de Gourgues recaptured San Mateo and executed the Spanish soldiers stationed there. But the Spanish continued to set up forts and Catholic **missions** all across the region of northern Florida.

The English were also interested in controlling Florida. In 1586, the English captain Sir Francis Drake looted and burned Saint Augustine, although Spain still controlled Florida and most of what is now the southeastern section of the United States. The English wanted more land and gradually captured it from the Spanish.

The Struggle to Win Florida

In 1702, English colonists in the Carolinas attacked Spanish Florida and again destroyed the town of Saint Augustine. But the Spanish fort there—Castillo de San Marcos—remained under Spain's control. The English colonists continued to take Spanish lands from Tallahassee to Saint Augustine. They destroyed Spanish

missions and killed or enslaved many Native Americans. The French, from their colony in Louisiana, pushed against Spanish Florida's western border. The French captured Pensacola in 1719. This was a mere twenty-one years after the town had been established. After years of attacks from the British and French, Spain's power in the region had weakened. The British continued to move southward. By 1733, Georgia, which bordered Spanish Florida, was the southernmost British colony. Colonists living in Georgia continued to extend the colony's borders and fight the Spanish in Florida.

During the mid-1700s, Britain and France fought each other in North America in a conflict called the French and Indian War. Spain sided with the French during some of the fighting. When the war ended with a British victory in 1763, France lost almost all its land in eastern North America. The British took control of this land. During the war, the British had captured Havana on the island of Cuba,

The French and Indian War lasted from 1754 to 1763.

Andrew Jackson's legacy includes terrible mistreatment of Native Americans.

which had been controlled by Spain. Spain traded Florida to Britain in order to get back Havana. The British now controlled Florida.

Britain split Florida into two colonies. East Florida's capital was Saint Augustine. Pensacola was the capital of West Florida. British control of the two Floridas lasted until Spanish troops marched back into West Florida during the American Revolution, which lasted from 1775 to 1783. The British surrendered parts of Florida to Spain in 1781. After they lost the war, the British gave up all of Florida to Spain. In 1783, Spain was once again in control of Florida.

But the end of the American Revolution was not an end to war in the region. Much of Florida still saw fighting. After the Revolutionary War, Britain continued to encourage Native Americans, including the Seminole and Creek, to fight against American settlers. The British provided the Native Americans with supplies and weapons to aid in these fights. The War of 1812, a result of unresolved problems between the United States and Britain, also brought unrest to the area.

Some Americans in the Southern states, whose economies depended on African American slave labor, were not pleased with Spanish control of Florida. They knew slaves could flee across the border to freedom there. Many of these escaped slaves joined with the Seminole. Americans in Georgia especially, as well as the federal government, were interested in making Florida part of the United States. Spanish control over Florida was weak, so American troops continued to push into Florida. These troops engaged in fighting against Native Americans and African Americans there. This fighting escalated into the First Seminole War (1817–1818). During this war, American general Andrew Jackson commanded the troops that fought the Seminole and African Americans and captured

major Spanish settlements. Under an 1819 treaty, Spain agreed to give Florida to the United States. It officially became part of the United States in 1821, and Andrew Jackson served as the territorial governor for a few months.

Seminole women and children on a reservation in Florida

The Path to Statehood

After Florida became a territory, the two Floridas were combined. Tallahassee became the new capital. Established in 1824, the city was chosen because it was halfway between the former capitals of Saint Augustine and Pensacola.

But peace did not come to Florida. As more and more people moved to the new territory, the white settlers decided they wanted Native American land. They also wanted escaped slaves removed from their Florida lands. In 1835, the Second Seminole War broke out between the US government and the Seminole people, who did not want to leave their homeland and relocate west of the Mississippi River. By that time, Andrew Jackson was the president of the

Important People in Florida's History

Walt Disney

One of the most famous people of Florida never lived in the state for long. Disney oversaw the construction of Disney World—Florida's most popular attraction. But he passed away before the amusement park was finished.

Thomas Edison

The famous inventor who created the first widespread lightbulb has deep ties to Florida. For fifty years, his family spent part of the year in Fort Myers, Florida. On his vast estate, Edison created a laboratory that studied plants. The tropical climate of Florida was well-suited to his research.

Thomas Edison

Henry Flagler

This industrialist helped create the Florida we know today. After he went on a honeymoon to Saint Augustine, he decided to build a railroad down the state. It stretched all the way down through the Florida Keys. Tourists could now travel more easily. He also built hotels across the state.

Ernest Hemingway

The famous author lived in the Florida Keys for many years. His house is now a museum. During his time there, he wrote a novel called *To Have and Have Not* that is set in the Keys. It focuses on the plight of a poor boat captain during the Great Depression.

Ernest Hemingway

Zora Neale Hurston

Hurston is one of the most famous writers of a literary movement called the Harlem Renaissance. Her books, stories, and poems are celebrated today as masterpieces that describe the African American experience in the early twentieth century. Hurston was raised in Eatonville, Florida.

Pedro Menéndez de Avilés

Born into a poor noble family, Menéndez de Avilés became an important admiral in the Spanish fleet. He was chosen to lead the expedition to found a colony at Saint Augustine. He defeated a nearby French settlement and secured Florida for the Spanish crown.

Juan Ponce de León

This famous conquistador was a key figure in early American history. It is believed he may have been on Christopher Columbus's second voyage to the New World. Ponce de León later became a Spanish governor and explored the Caribbean. His search for gold led him to colonize Puerto Rico and later to land on Florida's coast.

Zora Neale Hurston

Hernando de Soto

After sailing to the New World at the age of fourteen, de Soto rose to fame. He helped conquer parts of Central and South America on Spanish expeditions. In 1539, he arrived in Florida at the head of an army. He battled his way across the state and then farther inland. His men were the first Europeans to see the Mississippi River. It took some three years into their trek across the region to get there.

Harriet Beecher Stowe

Stowe is a famous author who is best known for her work *Uncle Tom's Cabin*. The novel records the evils of slavery. It caused great controversy when it was published. However, Stowe also wrote about other topics, like the beauty of Florida. She owned a home there that she returned to most winters.

Harriet Beecher Stowe

Abraham Lincoln was elected president in 1860.

United States. The war ended in 1842, and the Seminole were forced off their land. Some left by choice, while some were captured and sent to **reservations** in the West. Others escaped and made new lives in Florida's Everglades.

In 1845, Florida became the twenty-seventh state. By 1850, the state's population had reached 87,445. In 1855, Florida's legislature passed the Internal Improvement Act. Public land was offered to people who wanted to build businesses in Florida. Some transportation-industry businesses moved to Florida because of this act. The Third Seminole War (1855–1858) resulted in the forced relocation of more Seminole members to the West.

The Civil War

From when the British first established colonies in North America, Southern plantation owners relied on African American slaves to work their fields. To many white Southerners, this was their way of life. Without slaves, crops could not be grown, sold, or traded. White landowners in the South would lose money. Florida had many of these plantations.

The Northern way of life was different. The North's economy did not depend on large plantations. Some antislavery states in the North thought that the slave states in the South were too powerful. Many Northerners also felt that slavery was morally wrong.

Most Florida voters were not against slavery. When Abraham Lincoln ran for president in 1860, many Floridians disagreed with his politics. Many especially disagreed with his antislavery position. However, Lincoln won the election. On January 10, 1861, Florida seceded, or withdrew, from the Union (another name for the United States at the time). Florida was one of the eleven states that left the Union and joined together to form the Confederate States of America. These events led to the Civil War.

Though very few Civil War battles were fought on Florida soil, Union forces occupied many of the coastal towns and forts. The center of the state remained part of the Confederacy, though. Florida provided about fifteen thousand troops to the Confederate war effort, although more than two thousand Floridians fought for the North. The state also provided many supplies, including salt, beef, pork, and cotton, to the Confederate army. In the end, the South was defeated. Union troops took over the capital city of Tallahassee on May 10, 1865. Florida was once again part of the United States, though it was not officially readmitted to the Union as a state until 1868.

Reconstruction was a period of time during which the United States addressed the destruction of the Civil War, like the damage shown here.

Reconstruction

After so many years of fighting, Florida and other Southern states were in bad shape. The war had damaged their economies, and relations between Southerners and Northerners were poor. African Americans in the South still faced many problems. Many white people did not want to treat black people equally. After the Civil War, the federal government passed laws to protect the rights of black people. At the end of 1865, the Thirteenth Amendment to the US Constitution, abolishing slavery in the United States, was **ratified**. With help from the federal government, Southern states set up new state governments, rejoined the Union, and began to restore their economies. Slowly, the South was rebuilt.

During the late nineteenth century, Florida's economy grew stronger. Cattle raising became an important industry. So did growing citrus fruits such as oranges, grapefruits, and lemons. The Florida orange was becoming famous. The

Make Your Own Coral Reef

Florida is the only state in the continental United States with tropical coral reefs. They are a popular attraction for tourists. They are also an important part of the natural environment. Reefs are made up of millions of different creatures, including corals. Corals create hard skeletons out of calcium. These skeletons protect them and also form the structure of the reef. You can create your own corals at home!

Supplies

- A bag of brightly colored pipe cleaners
- A shallow box
- White sand

Directions

1. Twist two or three pipe cleaners together to make a thick branch of coral.
2. Wrap one end of a pipe cleaner to the thick branch to make a small branch.
3. Combine many different pipe cleaners together of different thicknesses. You can create a large, complex structure—just like real corals. To make your coral reef look more lifelike, you can make many corals with different colors.
4. Once you are happy with your corals, put some white sand in a shallow box.
5. Place the corals upright in the sand. You might need to anchor the bottom of your coral to make it stand upright.

growth of these industries throughout the state prompted the construction of many roads and railroads.

By the early 1900s, Florida's population and wealth were increasing. The invention and popularity of automobiles made it even easier for people to travel to Florida. Many stayed on and contributed to the state's growth. But the good times did not last.

American soldiers fight in a trench in Germany during World War I.

Two World Wars

World War I lasted from 1914 to 1918. In 1917, the United States entered the war, joining several other countries—including France, Great Britain, Russia, and Italy—to fight against Germany, Austria-Hungary, and the Ottoman Empire. Florida provided supplies to the war effort. Many Floridians served in the military at this time. The 1920s were difficult for Florida. Powerful hurricanes hit the state in 1926 and 1928. These storms killed so many fruit trees and destroyed so many homes and businesses that Florida's economy was badly hurt. Then, in 1929, Mediterranean fruit flies invaded many parts of the state. These pests destroyed crops. The citrus business was hit hard. Army troops set up roadblocks to stop people from bringing more infected fruit into the state. Florida's citrus production was reduced by more than half.

That same year, the entire country saw the beginning of what came to be called the Great Depression. Banks closed, and many businesses

FAST FACT

It was World War II that resulted in the widespread production of sunscreen. A pharmacist from Miami by the name of Benjamin Green created a cream to protect US airmen (like himself) from the sun. After the war, he started the company Coppertone to market his creation to the general public.

This family from Tennessee moved to Winterhaven, Florida, during the Great Depression.

failed. Workers lost their jobs, and many families did not have enough money for food. People stopped traveling. Florida's railroad companies were hurt. Florida was already experiencing hard times. The Great Depression, which lasted for about ten years, made the situation even worse.

After Japanese warplanes bombed the US naval base at Pearl Harbor, Hawaii, in 1941, the United States entered World War II, joining the fight against the governments of Germany, Japan, and Italy. World War II had already begun in Europe in 1939. It would last until 1945. Once again, Florida provided necessary supplies for the troops. As in World War I, Floridians served in the military. Because of its warm climate, Florida became a major training center for US soldiers, sailors, and pilots. More highways and airports were built to accommodate the increased traffic. These roads and airports became useful after the war, helping Florida's economy to grow.

Postwar Boom

Construction in Miami shows that Florida is full of economic opportunity.

Florida has experienced enormous population growth since World War II. Once one of the least populated and developed states in the nation, Florida became, by the turn of the twenty-first century, the country's fourth most populous state. (It later grew to become the third most populous state.) This growth occurred because Florida had a desirable climate and inexpensive land. The state was seen as a welcoming place. Throughout the state's history, tourism has always played an important role. But in the last part of the twentieth century, Florida tourism boomed. Thanks in large part to the opening of Walt Disney World, near Orlando, in 1971, Florida became the family vacation hot spot of the world. Visitors came for the theme parks as well as Florida's sunny beaches. Tourists wanted to see unique natural sites such as the Everglades and the Florida Keys. Through the years, many people have come to explore the islands. Visitors enjoy swimming in the warm waters, seeing the coral reefs, and taking part in offshore fishing.

Florida became a major tourist destination after World War II.

The citrus and fishing industries continued to bring money into the state. Mining and the new space and military technology industries also contributed to Florida's newfound prosperity. More businesses provided thousands of jobs.

Like other states, Florida was severely affected by the bad economic times that hit the country hard beginning in 2008. Many workers lost their jobs, and some people could not afford to stay in their homes. The tourism industry was also hurt because fewer Americans had money to travel. Financial support from the federal government helped Florida's government and people cope with these problems.

Hurricane Irma Makes History

Florida's coastal location demonstrates how a state's geography can shape its history. With the Atlantic Ocean on one side and the Gulf of Mexico on the other, Florida has experienced a number of tropical storms. Hurricane Andrew hit the state in August 1992, killing more than forty people in Florida. On September 10, 2017, Hurricane Irma made landfall. The storm left millions without power. It caused billions of dollars of damage. It also killed more than twenty people. Yet the people of Florida pulled together to evacuate and help each other. The state has always bounced back from bad storms.

The Tragedy at Stoneman Douglas High School

On February 14, 2018, seventeen high school students and teachers were killed in a shooting at Stoneman Douglas High School in Parkland. The tragedy brought the community together to discuss how to keep students all over the country safer. Student activists planned protests and gave interviews. These young people showed the power citizens have to shape the state and national government. Their goal was to make sure that no other students have to experience a tragedy like the one they went through.

A Bright Future

Recently, Florida has seen continued population and economic growth. In 2017, its population grew by more than one thousand people every day. Job opportunities in Florida draw people from around the country and the world. Experts believe its fast growth will continue in the future as more and more people choose to make Florida their home.

FAST FACT
Between August 2016 and June 2017, there was an outbreak of Zika virus in southern Florida. (The Caribbean and Latin America experienced the outbreak too.) While symptoms in adults are mild, the virus can seriously harm unborn babies. Fortunately, the virus was contained, and the outbreak is now over in Florida.

Two Florida high school students volunteer together.
Young people are one-fifth of Florida's population.

3 Who Lives in Florida?

Florida is the third most populous state (after California and Texas). More than twenty million people live there. Unlike most states, most Floridians were not born in Florida. Instead, they moved to the state from overseas or from other states in the country. In fact, 8 percent of Floridians were born in New York! This has led to a huge amount of diversity in Florida. People from all different backgrounds come to the state to make a new home for themselves.

Native Americans

The original Native Americans of Florida include the Timucua, Calusa, Apalachee, and Tequesta tribes. People in these tribes were killed by disease or warfare, captured as slaves, or forced by the Spanish to leave Florida. The Seminole people, descendants of many Native American tribes, had first come to Florida in the 1700s in search of new places to build homes. By the 1850s, when the United

FAST FACT
Some retirees come to Florida just for the winter months. This lets them avoid snow and cold weather in the North. An informal name for this group is "snowbirds." Snowbirds might rent or own a second house in Florida. Others drive down in recreational vehicles (RVs) that double as their home.

The Ah-Tah-Thi-Ki Museum is located on the Big Cypress Seminole Indian Reservation.

States declared an end to conflicts with the Seminole, thousands of Native Americans had been moved to reservations in the western United States. Some Seminole individuals remained in Florida by living in the swamps where American soldiers and settlers could not find them. Most of today's Seminole tribe members in Florida are the descendants of these people. Today, the state has six Seminole reservations. Several thousand Native Americans live on these reservations. The largest reservation is the Big Cypress Reservation. It has many attractions for visitors who want to learn about Seminole history.

The Seminole have developed a strong economy to support their way of life. Tourism is one way the Seminole earn money. The Seminole have a cultural museum as well as other tourist attractions, such as ecotours of the Florida Everglades. Visitors come to the reservations to enjoy these sites and learn more about Seminole culture. Tourists also visit the reservations' casinos. Many of today's Seminole make a successful living in the citrus and cattle industries. The money that comes from tourism and agriculture helps pay for Seminole schools and health care.

The Seminole also try to keep their traditions alive. They design some buildings like their ancestors' palm-thatched homes called chickees, although they do not live in them anymore. Many Seminole wear colorful patchwork clothing of the past. Storytelling is an important part of the culture, so Seminole legends are passed down from old to young. The Seminole are eager to share their history and culture with others. Some visit schools in different parts of Florida to teach students about their traditions and their long history in the state. The Seminole also share their culture at the state's many Native American festivals.

Fidel Castro died in 2016. He was Cuba's leader for nearly fifty years.

Cuban Americans

About 80 percent of Floridians were born in the United States. Of those born outside the United States, the largest number come from the neighboring island of Cuba. In 1959, Fidel Castro came to power and established a Communist government in Cuba. Since then, many Cubans have come to the United States to enjoy freedoms and economic opportunities not available in their own country. At certain times, the US government has welcomed Cuban refugees. At other times, US government policy has made it difficult for Cubans to enter the country legally. The Cuban government has generally not allowed people to leave Cuba legally. Over the years, many Cubans have left their country secretly. They have traveled to Florida on small, tightly packed boats or rafts. Crossing the water to Florida's shores is dangerous. Not all passengers have survived the journey.

In 1980, Castro's government let about 125,000 Cubans leave the country. Many traveled to

Florida's Celebrities

Antonio Brown

Antonio Brown was born in Miami in 1988. He has been a wide receiver for the Pittsburgh Steelers since 2010. In 2016, Brown competed on *Dancing with the Stars*.

Josh Gad

Actor Josh Gad was born in Hollywood, Florida, in 1981. He has found success on both the stage and on the big screen. Gad has been nominated for a Tony Award and has won a Grammy. In 2013, he lent his voice to *Frozen*'s snowman, Olaf.

Josh Gad

Ariana Grande

Born in Boca Raton, Grande is a singer and actress. She rose to fame for her role in the Nickelodeon show *Victorious*. After the show, she quickly launched a successful career as a singer. She has been nominated for four Grammy Awards.

Eva Mendes

Mendes was born in Miami to Cuban parents. Her career in acting was an accident. A casting agent happened to see her photo in the portfolio of a friend and contacted her. She appeared in a number of low-budget films. In 2001, her big break came in a commercially successful movie. Since then, she has had a successful acting and modeling career in Hollywood.

Ariana Grande

Maya Rudolph

Actress and comedian Maya Rudolph was born in Gainesville in 1972. In 2000, she became a member of the *Saturday Night Live* cast. Her success on the show led to roles in major movies. Rudolph has also voiced characters in animated films, such as Cass in *Big Hero 6* and Smiler in *The Emoji Movie*.

The Mariel Boatlift took place in 1980.

the Miami area in small boats, some of which were provided by Cuban Americans. This event became known as the Mariel Boatlift after the name of a Cuban port. A small number of the refugees had been released from Cuban jails. Because of this, some Floridians at first did not trust the new arrivals. They worried that they would not know the difference between criminals and law-abiding Cubans. This tension made it more difficult for many of the Cubans to find jobs and acceptance.

Today, the Cuban American community in Florida is thriving. Well over one million Cuban Americans play a major role in the state's economy, cultural life, and politics. A number of Cuban Americans have been elected to the US Congress. The largest concentration of Cuban Americans is in the Miami area. In fact, a part of Miami is called Little Havana. (Havana is Cuba's capital city.) Relations between the United States and Cuba have recently thawed somewhat. In 2009, President Barack Obama lifted travel restrictions to Cuba for Cuban Americans. The changes made it easier for Cuban Americans to

Calle Ocho is a street in Little Havana.

FAST FACT

Miami is one of the largest American cities where a majority of the population speaks Spanish. In fact, close to 70 percent of people in Miami identify as Hispanic. Most are Cuban American, but more and more Hispanics from different places are coming to Miami. As a result, the city has a vibrant culture and is known around the world for its unique diversity.

visit. It also got easier for Cuban Americans to send money to family members still living in Cuba. In 2016, President Obama even visited Cuba. He was the first sitting president to visit in more than eighty years. However, in June 2017, President Donald Trump announced he would again make it more difficult for Americans to visit Cuba. Trump also created rules preventing American people and companies from doing business with any company tied to the Cuban government during visits.

African Americans in Florida

Florida is home to many African Americans. Some black Floridians have come from other states or countries. Others have lived in Florida for generations.

A community, later known as Overtown, was set up in the northwestern section of Miami in 1896. At that time, laws in the South forced black people and white people to live separately. African Americans who worked in Miami lived in this part of town. Some of them worked in hotels, on the railroads, or in other businesses in Miami. Over the years, their hard work helped develop Miami and surrounding areas.

African Americans in Overtown were proud of their community. They had schools, businesses, and churches. In the 1960s, laws outlawing **segregation** were passed. Many people who were living in Overtown chose to leave, but some stayed. Today, efforts are being made to revitalize Overtown and to remind people of its successes and historical importance.

Retirees

Floridians come from all different walks of life. A large portion of the population has relocated from other states, including many people who have chosen to retire in Florida. Retirement homes and communities in Florida are very popular. Many retirees come to the state to enjoy the weather and relax. They may be from different ethnic and economic backgrounds. What they have in common is an appreciation for the Sunshine State.

Overtown residents are working hard to bring recognition to their community.

Florida's excellent golf courses are just one draw for retirees.

Immigration from Around the World

Throughout American history, millions of immigrants have come to this country from around the world. Individuals have had different reasons for uprooting their families and leaving home. Often, it was because life in their native country was unbearable due to violence or poverty. Other times, they simply yearned to live in a country with more opportunity.

Florida's history is defined by its immigrants. Nearly one in five Floridians was born outside the United States. Many more are second-generation immigrants. This means they are people whose parents were born abroad. While these immigrants come from places around the world, 75 percent are from the Caribbean and Latin America. The biggest group is from Cuba. In fact, 23 percent of all foreign-born Floridians are from Cuba. But many other countries have contributed large communities of immigrants to Florida's diverse population.

People from many Caribbean countries have come to Florida over the years. Jamaicans and Haitians have moved to Florida in large numbers. These two countries are notable because their populations do not speak Spanish, unlike most other Caribbean countries. Jamaicans speak English. Haitians speak Haitian Creole, a mixture of French and other languages. (France used to control Haiti.) Creole also has a large African influence since most Haitians are descended from Africans. These Africans were taken from their homes and sold into slavery.

Little Haiti, Miami

This map shows Florida in relation to Caribbean countries.

The Haitian community in South Florida is huge. More than 3 percent of the people in and around Miami were born in Haiti. This is the largest population of Haitians of any American city. One neighborhood in Miami is known as Little Haiti. The neighborhood is home to many restaurants that serve authentic Haitian food. There are also cultural attractions and museums that

A mural in Little Haiti

celebrate Haiti and its people. If you visit, you're likely to hear people speaking Haitian Creole.

Of course, the language other than English you are most likely to hear in Florida is Spanish. Immigrants and their descendants from Cuba and the Dominican Republic, as well as Central and South American countries, mostly speak Spanish. It used to be that the majority of Spanish-speaking immigrants in Florida came from Cuba. This was very different from the rest of the United States where most Spanish-speaking immigrants came from Mexico and other countries outside the Caribbean. Florida's large population of Cuban immigrants was unique within the country. This was a result of how close it was to Cuba.

In recent years, Florida's Spanish-speaking immigrant population has changed. Cuban-born immigrants are no longer in the majority of new arrivals. Immigration from Mexico, Central America, and Puerto Rico (part of the United States) has increased. As a result, the Hispanic culture in Miami and other cities is much more diverse now.

Key Lime Pie

Florida's state pie is delicious and easy to make. It is a two-step process. First, you need to make the crust. Then, you can work on the filling.

Crust

Crust Ingredients

- 1½ cups of crumbled graham cracker
- 5 tablespoons of butter
- 3 tablespoons of sugar

Directions

1. Preheat the oven to 350°F (176°C).
2. Mix the ingredients in a bowl and pack the mixture into a 9-inch (22.8 cm) pie plate. Make sure the crust covers the bottom and sides of the dish.
3. Bake the crust for ten minutes—it should turn golden brown.

Filling

Filling Ingredients

- 1 14 oz can of sweetened, condensed milk
- 4 egg yolks
- ½ cup of key lime juice
- Whipped cream (for topping)

Directions

1. Whisk the ingredients together until they are smooth.
2. Pour the liquid into the pie crust and bake for fifteen minutes at 350°F (176°C).
3. Take the pie out of the oven and let it cool.
4. Cover and refrigerate the pie until it is cold. Serve with whipped cream as a topping.

People who are sixty-five or older make up 19 percent of Florida's population. That is higher than any other state. In some areas popular with retirees, this number can climb even higher. In Sumter County, 52.9 percent of residents are sixty-five or older. It is the only county in the United States with a majority of senior citizens.

Education in Florida

Education is an important issue for many Floridians. Florida's education system has seen great improvements since the late 1990s. The high school graduation rate for the 2016–2017 school year was 82.3 percent. Reading and math scores have been on the rise. Many say Florida's success is thanks to the A+ Plan. One part of the plan helps identify schools with underperforming students. These schools get money to improve resources to help students perform at grade level. Another feature of the plan rewards teachers whose students show big improvements on statewide tests. The goal is to make sure that all of Florida's students have the chance to excel. In 2008, the US Department of Education chose Florida to participate in something called the Differentiated Accountability Pilot Project. Since then, differentiated accountability has helped the state provide assistance to schools that need it most.

Florida has a vast college and university system. The State University System of Florida includes twelve schools around the state. Florida also has dozens of private colleges, universities, and community colleges.

Increasing Diversity

As Florida's population continues to increase rapidly, its diversity is also growing. Experts

FAST FACT

Florida has the third-largest Jewish community of any state (after New York and California). A large part of the community is retirees and their families who moved to the state. However, Jewish immigrants also flock to the Sunshine State from around the world. Thousands of Spanish-speaking Jews from Latin America have come to the state in recent years.

Florida State University in Tallahassee is one of many public universities in the state.

think that by 2028, Florida will be become majority-minority. This means that the groups that are considered minority groups today will make up more than 50 percent of the population. As a result, Florida politics are expected to change. Currently, Florida is a swing state. This means that it is hard to predict which political party more Floridians will vote for in an election. As its minority population increases, however, the state is expected to lean more Democratic. This could have a big impact on national politics.

Florida's Biggest Colleges and Universities

1. University of Central Florida, Orlando (shown above)
(55,776 undergraduate students)

(All enrollment numbers are from US News and World Report 2018 rankings.)

2. Florida International University, Miami
(45,813 undergraduate students)

3. University of Florida, Gainesville
(34,554 undergraduate students)

4. Florida State University, Tallahassee
(32,929 undergraduate students)

5. University of South Florida, Tampa
(31,461 undergraduate students)

6. Florida Atlantic University, Boca Raton
(25,402 undergraduate students)

Florida State University

7. Indian River State College, Fort Pierce
(18,244 undergraduate students)

8. Keiser University, Fort Lauderdale
(18,172 undergraduate students)

9. Seminole State College of Florida, Sanford
(17,788 undergraduate students)

University of Florida, Gainesville

10. Florida SouthWestern State College, Fort Myers
(16,616 undergraduate students)

Florida is known worldwide for its citrus crops. Here, workers stand on ladders to pick lemons.

4 At Work in Florida

Florida is home to many different kinds of businesses. From family-owned farms to high-tech manufacturing, the state does it all. The tourism industry and the service industry that support it are especially important in the Sunshine State. Hotels, restaurants, banks, and the many other businesses that make tourism possible employ many Floridians. But Florida is also on the cutting edge of innovation. Its many universities partner with local tech companies to create exciting new products.

The Tourism Industry

Florida's economy relies heavily on tourism. Many Florida businesses depend on the money tourists spend. Many Florida workers provide goods and services to visitors. Also, the state government depends on tourism for a significant portion of the state's tax revenue. This is because Florida has no state income tax. People who live and work in Florida do not have to give part of the money they earn (their income) to the state. The lack of income tax is one reason that the state is so popular

FAST FACT!
Florida is an important hub of international trade. Its long coastline supports a number of ports. Ships export goods from across the United States to markets in Latin America and the Caribbean. This huge amount of trade is responsible for an estimated million jobs in the state.

Magic Kingdom is one of several Disney theme parks in Florida.

for retirees. Their retirement savings go further when there is no state income tax.

The major way that the state collects money for government programs is through the state sales tax. The sales tax is added to goods and services sold in the state. The state collects this money from the companies that sell the goods and services. Florida residents pay a large part of the sales tax, of course. But if tourists did not come to the state to stay in hotels or campgrounds, eat in restaurants, shop in stores, and more, the state of Florida would collect less money to pay for government services.

Out-of-state visitors spent $108.8 billion in Florida in 2015. In Florida's tourist industry, Disney is tops. Walt Disney World brings money and jobs into the state. Because of Disney's success, other theme parks have been built in the Orlando area. Hotels have sprung up there and elsewhere in the state to give the tourists a place to stay. Cruise ships dock in Florida ports every day, bringing many tourist dollars into the state.

Throughout the year, tourists take advantage of the state's warm weather and outdoor activities. Florida's beaches are very popular. Some people visit the Everglades to see the state's wildlife. The Florida Keys are also an appealing destination. The islands are ideal for snorkeling, diving, swimming, fishing, exploring the tropical wilderness, visiting historic sites, or enjoying the local events. Many tourists visit the Kennedy Space Center at Cape Canaveral to learn about space exploration.

A chance to meet beloved Disney characters brings millions of tourists to Florida.

Agriculture and Mining

Tourism is not the only way people and companies in the state of Florida make money. Raising **livestock** is important. And while agriculture was the state's first major industry, it continues to be important today. Florida is the second-largest agricultural state in the southeast, after North Carolina. In 2014, agricultural exports were worth $4 billion.

Today, agriculture is still a key sector of Florida's economy.

The star of agriculture in Florida is the orange. Florida ranks first among all states in orange juice production. Meanwhile, farmers harvest peanuts and pecans in northern Florida. Cauliflower, broccoli, and sweet corn also grow in Florida. In February and March, boxcars filled with winter produce head north out of Florida. This produce includes snap beans, squash, celery, and tomatoes. These foods ship mostly to states where the winters are cold and the growing seasons are short. Florida leads the nation in the

Florida Oranges

Florida is known around the world for its oranges. Nearly 90 percent of the oranges grown in Florida are processed into juice, rather than sold fresh. As a result, Florida produces more orange juice than any country other than Brazil. This is despite the fact it is a state and not a country!

Oranges were not native to the Americas before the arrival of the Europeans. But early explorers brought oranges with them and planted orange trees soon after they arrived. In Florida, the first orange trees were planted at Saint Augustine in the mid-1500s. The state's climate was perfect for the imported trees. Soon after their arrival, wild orange trees could be found around the state.

It was not until the 1800s that orange production in Florida became a large business. Groves of oranges were planted in the north of the state and shipped to the rest of the country. After the Civil War ended in 1865, railroads were built in Florida and the industry grew quickly. But in 1894 and 1895, disaster struck. Two freezes hit the state, killing most of the orange trees. Many people in the industry gave up and left the state. However, others stayed and replanted their groves farther south in Florida. The industry eventually rebounded.

The popularity of frozen concentrate orange juice skyrocketed in the 1940s. Growers switched to juicier varieties of oranges as juice became more profitable. Since then, orange juice production has dominated the industry.

The history of oranges and other citrus, like grapefruits, has not always been easy in Florida. Problems like frost, diseases, and pests have threatened orange groves time and again. The most recent problem is a disease called citrus greening. Spread by an insect, the disease first occurred in Florida in 1998. It continues to plague the state and kill orange trees. As of 2016, orange production in the state had dropped more than 65 percent over just twenty years due to the disease. But farmers have banded together to fight its spread.

The Florida's Natural brand started in 1933.

The orange on the right suffers from citrus greening.

sale of many major fruits and vegetables. Among other types of fruit, Florida farms grow oranges, grapefruits, strawberries, mangoes, watermelons, tangerines, limes, and tangelos. Farmers also grow vegetables such as peppers, sweet corn, cucumbers, and beans. Because of year-round warm weather, the state also provides the rest of the country with houseplants, ferns, and flowers.

Florida farmers grow more than citrus. Strawberries are also an important crop.

Florida is also the state that produces the most sugarcane. This cash crop was one reason that European countries sought to colonize the Americas. The tropical climate of some regions, like Florida, was well-suited to sugarcane. Today, most American sugar comes from sugar beets. But Florida is one of the few states to continue growing sugarcane.

Ranches around the state breed cattle for the beef industry. Cows are raised on dairy farms, as well. Ranchers also raise hogs and poultry.

Additionally, Florida is one of the leading suppliers of phosphate. Phosphate is mined in Florida and shipped to the rest of the country and around the world. Most phosphate is used to make plant fertilizers. Other products in which phosphate is used include food for farm animals.

FAST FACT!
Florida's climate is great for farming. Warm weather means the state's growing season is longer than in most of the country. Florida also receives a high average rainfall every year. This increases the yield of many crops and makes farming more profitable.

A technician works at a factory in Vero Beach.

Manufacturing

There are factories across Florida, although manufacturing plays a small role in the state's economy. At food-processing plants, many of the state's agricultural products, such as citrus fruits, are made into juices and jams. Paper mills also dot the state.

Companies in the state make equipment needed to run the space programs at Cape Canaveral. The state also has military and aerospace industries. New technology is developed at government labs. This technology is important for both space exploration and military defense.

The rocket garden at Kennedy Space Center

Protecting the Environment

Florida's population and economy have grown tremendously in recent decades. This growth has led to the construction of many homes, businesses, schools, and highways. It has increased demand for such things as water and electricity, as well as increasing the amount of waste to be disposed of. These and other changes have put pressure on the state's environment and natural

Agritech

Florida is at the cutting edge of agricultural technology, or agritech. Many different technologies are used to make agriculture more profitable. One example is automated harvesting using robotics. A firm in Florida is trying to create a robot to harvest strawberries. Currently, strawberries need to be picked by hand. If a robot could harvest them, it would make strawberries cheaper to produce.

High-Tech Innovation

New technologies are coming out of Florida's companies and universities all the time. One recent example is a new supercapacitor battery made by researchers from the University of Central Florida. If it becomes available commercially, phones could be charged in a matter of seconds.

Emerging Industries

Dragon fruit, or pitaya, finds a welcoming climate in Florida.

Modeling, Simulation, and Training

Florida is a world leader in the modeling, simulation, and training sector (MS&T). While the sector has been growing over the past seventy years, it is only recently that it exploded in popularity. Florida produces the simulations that allow people like pilots and soldiers to train before putting their skills to the test.

Nanotechnology

One new area of scientific research is nanotechnology. Nanotech is the manipulation of incredibly tiny particles. Scientists hope that it will revolutionize many different fields, like medicine and engineering. Florida is a global center for nanotech. Many international companies have offices in Florida to take advantage of the expertise available there.

Tropical Fruits

New tropical fruits are on the rise in Florida. One example is the pitaya (or dragon fruit), which can now be found in many supermarkets. In 2006, there were just 50 acres (20.2 hectares) devoted to pitaya production in Florida. In 2016, there were 500 acres (202 ha). It is hoped that as the popularity of tropical fruits grows, Florida's farmers will profit.

A biologist films a panther's release into its natural habitat in West Palm Beach.

resources. An issue for Floridians today is how to strike the right balance between continuing the state's growth and protecting its environment.

One of Florida's great natural resources is its coral reefs. Florida is the only place in the continental United States with a long line of coral reefs in its coastal waters. Coral reefs are underwater formations made up of both living and nonliving elements. The base of a coral reef is limestone. Most of this limestone is the skeletons of dead corals (a type of marine animal). Living corals make up the top of the reef, closest to the surface of the water. Coral reefs provide shelter and food for many underwater plants and animals. They also protect the land from waves from the ocean. Many medicines are made from plants and animals living on or among coral reefs.

Every year, thousands of scuba divers and snorkelers—both tourists and state residents— visit Florida's coral reefs. Some touch or step on the living corals. Broken or scraped corals can become infected and die. Boaters and fishers also accidentally start these infections when they hit the corals. Corals also need clear, clean water to grow. Water pollution from factories, cities, and farms has become a problem in Florida. Climate change is also taking its toll on coral reefs. As temperatures rise, the algae that live in corals die. Corals eat this algae. Without algae, corals are very weak. Other aspects of climate change make it difficult for corals to grow in the first place.

The state government and the US Coral Reef Task Force have tried to protect Florida's coral reefs, but they cannot do it alone. It is up to both residents and visitors to understand that in a matter of seconds they can destroy some of the rare beauty of a coral reef.

A State of Success

Florida's economy looks poised for more growth. Experts expect it will continue to grow more quickly than the national average. Its low tax rates and business-friendly laws make it an attractive place to start a business. This is good news if you want to move to the state. It means you will likely be able to find a job in Florida!

Florida's coral reefs need to be protected.

The Historic Capitol Building, now a museum, stands in front of the current, more modern capitol.

5 Government

Like all states, Florida has its own government. This government is free to make its own laws and govern as it sees fit. However, the laws it makes must line up with the US Constitution and laws passed by Congress (which apply to all fifty states).

Florida also has a number of local governments in its counties and cities. These governments can also make their own laws and regulations. Local laws must also be in line with national and state laws.

Separation of Powers

The state government of Florida is organized into three branches. The **executive** branch is headed by the governor. The **legislative** branch makes the state's laws, and the **judicial** branch includes the state's courts.

The Executive Branch

The governor is the chief executive of the state of Florida. He or she serves a four-year term and cannot serve more than two terms

FAST FACT
There is a tradition in Florida that the state's governor commissions an official portrait as his or her term draws to a close. The state capitol has portraits of every governor since the 1890s. Though these portraits hang in the capitol, they are actually in the care of the Museum of Florida History.

The Florida Supreme
Court chamber

in a row. The governor is responsible for appointing the heads of many state government agencies and for appointing many of the state's judges. The governor also signs or rejects bills that may or may not become laws.

The Legislative Branch

Like most other states and the federal government, Florida's lawmakers are divided into two houses: the Florida Senate, with 40 members, and the Florida House of Representatives, with 120 members. Each legislator represents a certain part of the state. The residents from each district elect their own lawmakers. Senators serve four-year terms, while representatives serve two-year terms. Members of both houses must live in the district they represent and be at least twenty-one years old. They cannot hold office for more than eight years.

The Judicial Branch

The Florida courts decide whether someone accused of a crime has broken the law. They also settle disputes between individuals or companies. Most cases start in a trial, or circuit, court. Decisions of trial courts can be appealed to one of Florida's five district courts. District court decisions can be appealed to the state's highest court, the Florida Supreme Court, whose seven justices are appointed by the governor. After a trial period, Floridians vote every six years on whether or not a justice can continue serving on the court.

Creating New Laws

Every year, Florida's legislature meets to discuss the issues that are important to the people of the state. In recent years, those issues

Government is about people. Laws should reflect what the people of a state or country think. That's why it is important to stay involved in politics. As a citizen, your opinion counts.

You can use social media to learn about politics. One platform that is commonly used is Twitter. Politicians will often tweet about what they are doing. They might ask for support from the community they serve. They also might post important announcements online. For example, when hurricanes strike Florida, politicians tweet advice on how to stay safe.

There are many different Twitter accounts related to Florida politics. You can ask an adult to show you the Republican and Democratic Parties' accounts: @FloridaGOP and @FlaDems. You can also ask an adult to show you the Florida Senate Twitter account: @FLSenate. For accounts like this, the person in control might change from year to year. As of 2018, the Republicans have a majority in the state senate. That means they use the @FLSenate account. This will change if the Democrats win a majority at some point.

The current governor of Florida is Republican Rick Scott. He became governor in 2011. Governor Scott often tweets in both English and Spanish. This reflects Florida's diversity and ensures he reaches all Floridians. In January of 2019, Scott's term will end and he won't be governor. When that happens, the next governor will have his or her own account.

Keeping Up with Politics

Governor Rick Scott signs a bill into law.

The Florida Senate's official Twitter page

have included crime, education, the environment, and the economy. One recent law to come into effect was the Unmanned Aircraft Systems Act. It tried to regulate a new concern of the modern world: drones. The law forbids them from flying over some areas that are clearly restricted on the ground. For example, flying over pipelines and cell towers is forbidden.

Legislators decide whether new laws should be created or old laws changed. Suggestions for new laws can come from the state senate or the house. These suggestions are called bills. A committee discusses a proposed bill. Members of the committee can make changes to the bill, and the committee rejects or approves it. Once the committee has approved a bill, it goes to the entire house to review. Like the committee, the entire house can change the bill, and it then rejects or approves the bill.

Both houses must approve a bill before it can become a law. A bill passed in one house goes to the other house for review. Once both houses approve the bill, it goes to the governor, who can sign and approve the bill, or reject—or veto—it. If the governor approves the bill, it becomes a law. If the governor vetoes the bill, the state legislature can override the veto with a two-thirds majority in both houses. If the governor takes no action, the bill becomes a law after sixty days.

In 2017, the legislature filed about 1,900 new bills. Just 234 were passed by the legislature and became law when Governor Rick Scott signed them.

A Changing Constitution

While you might imagine the Constitution of Florida is rather stable, like the US Constitution, it is not. Currently, the state is on its sixth constitution. Approved in 1968, Florida's constitution is subject to change all the time. In fact, there are five different ways the constitution can be changed. This is more than any other state constitution. For example, every twenty years a Constitution Revision Commission suggests changes to the constitution that are then voted on. Most recently, this occurred in 2017–2018. Citizens and lawmakers suggested many amendments to the constitution. Some related to giving more voting rights to people who have committed crimes in the past. Others related to simple text changes in the constitution, like removing text that described amendments that have been repealed. Many amendments were proposed on all kinds of issues.

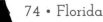

Glossary

bounty	Something that occurs in generous amounts.
commemorate	To mark and celebrate something, such as a date or person.
conquistador	Literally "conqueror" in Spanish; the name for the Spanish leaders who conquered the New World.
continental United States	The forty-eight states that do not include Hawaii and Alaska.
executive	The branch of government that is led by the president or governor.
geological	Relating to the study of Earth.
gullible	Easily fooled or tricked.
judicial	The branch of government that is made up of the courts.
legislative	The branch of government responsible for creating laws; in Florida, it is composed of the Florida House of Representatives and the Florida Senate.
livestock	Animals that are raised by people, such as cows, goats, and pigs.
missions	Outposts set up to spread Christianity among non-Christian populations.
moccasins	Shoes made of leather that were worn by Native Americans across much of North America.
peninsula	A landmass that is mostly surrounded by water.
ratified	Passed—in the sense of a law being passed.
reservations	Small areas of land that Native Americans were forced to move to when they were driven from their homelands.
segregation	Laws that separated whites and African Americans.
succored	Given help to.

Blackwater River State Forest
Britton Hill
Lake Seminole
Osceola National Forest
95
Timucuan Ecological & Historic Preserve

29
90
331
10
231
19
441
41
Jacksonville

98
319
Tallahassee
27
90
221
129
10
1

Pensacola
San Rosa I.
Panama City
98
Apalachicola National Forest
Apalachee Bay
St. Marks National Wildlife Refuge
75
301
St. Johns R.

ATLANTIC OCEAN

Apalachicola
Cape San Blas
St. Vincent National Wildlife Refuge
98
St. George Island
Lower Suwanee National Wildlife Refuge
Horseshoe Point
Gainesville
Ocala National Forest
17
Lake George
Daytona Beach
95

Chassahowitzka National Wildlife Refuge
19
Ocala
41
98
Daytona International Speedway
Canaveral National Seashore
John F. Kennedy Space Center

Suwannee R.
98
301
Withlacoochee State Forest
Titusville
Orlando
Cape Canaveral

Gulf of Mexico

19
41
75
Walt Disney World Resort
4
Kissimmee
192
Melbourne

Clearwater
Tampa
27
Lake Kissimmee
Florida's Turnpike
95

St. Petersburg
Tampa Bay
17
Kissimmee R.
441
98
Port St. Lu

Sarasota
27
Lake Okeechobee
1
St. Lucie Canal

Port Charlotte
41
Arthur R. Marshall L. National Wildlife
We

Charlotte Harbor
Caloosahatchee R.
75
Fort Myers
27
95
Coral
Ft.

Cape Coral
Sanibel I.
OKALOACOOCHEE SLOUGH
BIG CYPRESS SWAMP
75
Ho

Big Cypress National Preserve
41
Hialeah
M
Miami

Cape Romano
THE EVERGLADES
Biscay

Ponce de Leon Bay
Everglades National Par
Key La

Cape Sable
Florida Bay
1

Dry Tortugas National Park
Key West
FLORIDA KEYS

Dry Tortugas
Marquessas Keys

0   *miles*   **150**

N
W   E
S

	Interstate		State Capital		State Forest
	Major Highway		Highest Point in State		National Park
	Florida's Turnpike		Historic Site		National Wildli
	City or Town		National Forest		State Park
					Other Points of

Map Skills

1. What national forest is south of the state capital?

2. What body of water touches the western coast of Florida?

3. What is the southernmost national park on this map?

4. What river flows into Lake Okeechobee?

5. What point of interest is on Cape Canaveral?

6. To get to the Big Cypress Preserve from Miami, which highway would you take?

7. What is the westernmost city labeled on this map?

8. To get to Port Saint Lucie from Melbourne, what direction would you travel?

9. What interstate runs north–south through Florida?

10. What is special about Britton Hill?

Answers

1. Apalachicola National Forest
2. Gulf of Mexico
3. Dry Tortugas National Park
4. Kissimmee River
5. John F. Kennedy National Space Center
6. Highway 41
7. Pensacola
8. South
9. I-95
10. It is the highest point in the state

More Information

Books

Conklin, Wendy. *The Seminoles of Florida: Culture, Customs, and Conflict.* Huntington Beach, CA: Teacher Created Materials, 2016.

Marsico, Katie. *The Everglades.* Social Studies Explorer. Ann Arbor, MI: Cherry Lake Publishing, 2013.

Sammons, Sandra Wallus. *Henry Flagler: Builder of Florida.* Sarasota, FL: Pineapple Press, 2010.

Websites

A Brief History
http://dos.myflorida.com/florida-facts/florida-history/a-brief-history
Florida's Department of State outlines the history of Florida.

Everglades National Park
http://kids.nationalgeographic.com/explore/nature/everglades
National Geographic presents information about the Everglades.

Junior Ranger Program
https://www.floridastateparks.org/things-to-do/junior-ranger
Florida's state park website features a junior ranger toolkit with activities and resources.

Visit Florida
http://www.visitflorida.com
Florida's official tourism website shares information about exciting things to do in the state.

Index

Page numbers in **boldface** are illustrations. Entries in **boldface** are glossary terms.